HERON'S CANOE

MARK de BRITO

HERON'S CANOE

PEEPAL TREE

First published in 2003

Peepal Tree Press Ltd
17 King's Avenue
Leeds LS6 1QS

British Library CIP data:
de Brito, Mark Angelo
Heron's canoe
I. Title
821.914 (contemporary English poetry)

ISBN

Cover art: 'Birds in a tree' (2000) by Dada
(acrylic on canvas, 62cm x 90cm),
reproduced by permission of the Rebecca Hossack Gallery (London).

Photograph of the author by 'Spiri'.
Typeset by the author.
Printed and bound by Peepal Tree Press.

for Sylvia Chevalier

CONTENTS

FOREWORD

The 'argument' which follows overleaf is a guide to the whole poem. The purpose of the more copious 'notes' is to document sources and identify allusions. My intention is that the bibliography will have uses for readers beside its value in illuminating the context of this poem.

I am grateful to the Rebecca Hossack Gallery (London) for permission to reproduce the painting 'Birds in a tree' (2000) by Dada, a San artist of Botswana.

Portions of *Heron's Canoe* have previously appeared in the journals *Seshat*, *Wasafiri*, *Poetry London*, and *Ifá speaks*. I have also read parts of the work in Port-of-Spain, London, Sheffield, and Ile-Ifẹ.

MdeB

ARGUMENT

'Heron's canoe' is English for the Carib name of a constellation, which includes the stars of Ursa Major. The subject of the poem is Caribbean and African history. *Heron's Canoe* falls into three main parts, which comprise cantos I-VI, VII-XII, and XIII-XVI. The opening six cantos, an exposition of cultural domains of the whole, deal with points of origin, mythic and historical, and with collision between cultures.

I

¶   Peaks are seen; ends
          are not seen;
for end and outcome
          are yet to be,

lord of disclosure.
          When the oil-palm
dies, young fronds
          flap about the trunk.

It was said
          we should sacrifice
lest our travels
          bring forgetfulness.

Rite without fixity
          yet firm
on time's foundations:
          let the house

be strong, on strong
          foundations.

¶   Ilé Ifẹ̀, where tongues
          converge.
Each day we drift
          further from our self,

and the end
          is incomprehension.
How will separate soul
          know its home

in divinity? The mouth
      of Ọ̀ṣun is sweet
as sorrel: one drop
      waters a desert.

¶   The slender palm tree
      on the hill
twists and splits
      into sixteen huts.

Ifá was visiting Òjìgì.
      He was going to visit
the shrine of the earth,
      the day he found

the love-shrine of Ọ̀ṣun.
      Speaker of all
languages, witness of destiny,
      disguised as a woman,

Ọ̀rúnmìlà made love with Ọ̀ṣun
      at the river.
He began to dance, and she
      was rejoicing.

He said his diviners
      had spoken the truth.

¶   Struggle is ahead
      and exile's shore.

Earth's voice, Egúngún,
      dumb to reply,
becomes a straying bird
      or broken pot.

Ifá withdraws
  and rivers fail.
Our twin is denied
  and forests fall.

¶ Peaks are seen; ends
   are not seen;
for end and outcome
   are yet to be,

lord of disclosure.
   Truth is many,
and yet we end
   as we begin.

Three-horned chameleon
   with swivelling
eyes, map me a path
   in history's tatters.

Èṣù Bàrágbó o, mo júbà.

Ifá said: "Let's go.
   You must visit
the shrine of the earth.
   Let's go to Èṣù."

II

The secret of heaven
      is in the heavens;
the secret of earth
      is in the earth,

where four rivers flow
from a single source.

Let the garden stand
      open to the north
and to the east; let the
      scents be spread.

I shall serve, lady,
      none but you, whom
my soul has sought,
      and cries at your door:

Duce Dame, aïe, aïe,
Reïne Dame, ovrez, ovrez.

Let the garden stand
open to the north
and to the east.

Passe avant, traveller.

The *mappa mundi* will guide,
      circular icon
of God's plan, to order
      of papal Caesar,

eye's island rimmed
        with nature's contrary,
and further, death, where Christ
        sits in judgement.

Passe avant, traveller.

Begin at Jerusalem, walled
        city, world's
hub, and the Red Sea
        parts for passage;

in the north, those who see
        better by night;
in Africa, headless Blemmyes
        and anthropophagi;

west, the Pillars of Hercules;
        east, Gog and Magog,
the man-eating martikhora,
        and the island

encircled with flame, *el fin
        del Oriente*, Columbus'
parayso terrenal, to which an angel
        bars return.

Passe avant, traveller
        to Outremer.

The secret of heaven
        is in the heavens;
the secret of earth
        is in the earth.

Duce Dame, aïe, aïe,
Reïne Dame, ovrez, ovrez.

Let the garden stand
open to the north
and to the east.

III

¶ His name was Yaya, yet Yaya
      has no name, first
essence, Sirius, accidence
      of stars; edging

amnesia, his doubleness
      becomes two:
below: Attabeira, mother
      of waters, snake-

coiled in stone collars;
      above: Yúcahu,
cassava-giver, male
      without any before.

Rebel Yayael, son of Yaya,
      you were banished
four months, as maize
      ripens, then returned

to be sacrificed, your body
      dismembered, bones
heaped in a gourd, which Yaya
      hangs from his roof,

assassin of his son, at this
      first of funerals.
It was Deminán, *Alpha Orionis*,
      and his three brothers,

these four tamers of fire
      who with rough palms
split the gourd of Yaya,
      that the earth spread

its hands to the cardinal points,
    that seas flowed,
filling the earth. As the sun
    passes from dawn

to the house of Coaybay,
    Yayael, son
of Yaya, let your bones
    hang from my roof.

¶   Morning Pleiades emerge
    in May, spelling
rains. I, poor hermit,
    friar Ramón,

write what I have learnt
    of Taíno idolatries.
Evening Orion brings
    December drought.

To look into Guaccaiarima,
    genital cave
of the island of Haití, sill
    of interrupted

time. They took Christian
    images, buried them
for a charm: "Now your fruit
    will be good."

The malefactors were tried,
    and burnt.
Dog-spirit Opiyelguobirán
    escapes by night

from his shrine to the woods,
      where devotees
will search, and bind him
      once more.

Christ came, and the dog
      cannot be found,
end foretold, souls
      sent to Coaybay.

¶ Those who left the cave
      of the *jagua*-tree
became stones, trees, birds,
      until Guahayona

said to the women: "Let's go.
      Leave the west,
your husbands, your children,
      the mountain Cauta."

So they set out eastward
      in his canoe.
Father Guahayona,
      first navigator,

when the Heron's Canoe
      in Ursa Major
dips into the sea,
      April to August,

that is the time
      of distant journeys;
and that the trip
      should not stray,

you flung one-legged
    Anacacuya, whirlwind
companion, headlong
    from the canoe

into the sea: he dies
    to become the Pole Star,
guiding the round-trip
    to Guanín.

You visited Matininó where
    women remained,
and you reached Guanín, farthest
    point in the east,

source of the sacred
    alloy of the sun
and Venus. Returning west
    to Cauta,

Guahayona met Guabonito,
    lady of the sea:
she cured him of his syphilis,
    gave him charms

and jewels of the rainbow.
    He returned
home to his father and son,
    named anew.

IV

Anno Domini 1522. Book of the ship *Samta Maria da Comçeiçam*, which God save and guard and give good voyage, and which now goes

to gather a cargo in the Forcados river.

We sailed from the island of São Tomé on the twelfth of March, and arrived on the first of April, held up by south-westerlies.

The pilot bought 33 girls, 22 boys, 30 women, 34 men. Six corpses were cast into the sea.

For seven *cabras* of cowries, the pilot bought for the Church of *Nossa Senhora* the one slave due from every ship.

São Tomé, mould
    of Creole tongues.
To be refined sugar-
    white by Christ's

mill (in the *Explicación*
    of Antonio Nicolás);
to be torn from history
    and destiny.

Tell names of the ships,
    ἔσπετε νῦν μοι,
count the uncountable,
    Muses of memory:

    Santa Clara
    Saint Jan
    Jesus of Lubeck

Ìbà Olókun.
Praise to the sea.

La Vierge de Grâce
Marie Séraphique
Santa Maria da Conceição

Ìbà Olókun.
Praise to the sea.

Adventure
Swallow
Amitié
Amistad

Hail, Òṣun, protectress
of the lost ones
who cross the waters.

La Perle
Donna Paula
Scipio
Hannibal

Hail, Ògún, warrior,
master of insurrection.

Clotilde
Colombe
Atlantic
Windrush

Ìbà Olókun.
Praise to the sea.

São Tomé, unstanched
    wound of Africa.
To be shorn of past
    and future.

Signature of the clerk: Fernandez. We sailed from the Forcados
    on the 22nd of June. Rounding the Cabo Fermoso at
    night, we came upon a heavy storm.

V

Bida, child of earth,
     ancient guardian
of Wagadu-Ghana,
     promises rain

and gold of Bambuk
     in exchange
for a virgin, each year
     given in sacrifice.

Twenty-two kings
reigned before the Flight;
twenty-two after.

Black cobra, Bida,
     who sleep and are
reborn, if you ascend
     from your cave

to the sky, I ascend
     upon your brow.

From the *kishwar*-zone of Babil, middle clime of seven, we set
     out in quest of Ghana, where gold grows like carrots,

through realms of the Sudan of al-Bakri, which extends seven
     years' travelling, as far as the edge of Ocean.

Desert spreads across millennia: children of Ham disperse out
     of Babil towards the foundation of cities.

At the source of the Nile, rocks gleam like silver, Ptolemy's
     Mountains of the Moon, site of Trismegistos' dome.

Twin tributaries rise there: one flowing north to Egypt; the other west to Ghana – along its banks, ebony and tamarisk grow thick.

Wind dried up the water in the water-skins: we journeyed by dunes and deep sands, salt-merchants, meeting with marvels:

Those who sharpen their teeth to a needle-point; those who trade silent and unseen; worshippers of the sun, and Alexander's crows; those with eyes and mouths in their chests; the red-eyed king of the cannibal Damdam; the Lamlam, suitable slaves; tribes of women with narrow vaginas; those without law or religion, who scarcely understand speech; those whose brain has boiled in the sun; inhabitants of underground burrows; eaters of raw meat.

Killed by the suitor
      to a chosen virgin,
Bida uttered a curse
      of drought, scarce

gold, the insane *jihad*
      of Ibn Yasin.
Thus Wagadu-Ghana
      became desert.

If you ascend, Bida,
      from your cave
to the sky, I ascend
      upon your brow.

VI

One hymn is sung across
      earth and ships
of the sea, one consummation
      for scattered rites.

Praise to you, Isis of many
      names, lady
of Philae and the Abaton,
      sovereign of north

and south, who hold off
      life's gales,
rescuing those who sail
      through storms.

Kush and Egypt fallen, it was the Blemmyes, heirs to the old
      divinities, who resisted Christian empire

into the sixth century: despite the Theodosian Code, against all
      odds, Roman arms and edicts, proto-crusades, propaganda,

the Blemmyes maintained Isis' temple at Philae:

they continued to transport an image of the goddess by river-
      boat to the Abaton and back to Philae, according to
      ancient custom.

The ship of Isis
sails into blue mist.

Those above honour you;
those below respect you.

Anubis and Nephthys
pour milk in libation.

Circa 537 AD, on orders of Justinian, the Byzantine general
Narses closed the temple at Philae, arresting the last
priests.

The temple was converted by Bishop Theodore to a church of
St Stephen, first martyr.

Divine mother, lady of Philae,
        gather our limbs
to accomplishment, soul's
        boat-trip to Abydos.

VII

Mi ben skrifi da tori (Johannes
      King): I have written
our forefathers' story, how
      they suffered, at war

with Bakra, maroons who fled
      the brand of the *fleur-
de-lis*, outgunned, outnumbered,
      who yet planted

a garden in hostile forest,
      who yet kept faith
with the dream of *Afrikan kondre*,
      soul's insurrection,

as of arms, to build anew
      on another continent
the sacred city: *Gînê*,
      home of the gods,

island under the sea.
      Abydos: *axis mundi*.

I have written of our forefathers,
      the triumph of wars
won: *dem plij drom, dem dansi,
      dem bloo Afrikan*

trompeti, wooden trumpets
      of the *sanga* war-rites,
just as in Africa. They poured
      bush-rum on the earth

for the gods and ancestors
  who helped them fight.
Legba Pétro, Marinette
  Bwa-Chèch, Ogoû

Jé-Rouj, aid us now.
  To build a *quilombo*
of the word, pitching camp
  in a strange tongue.

I raise a black flag
  to honour the old-time
warriors, *dem ouloe fetiman*,
  fighters for freedom:

Ganga Zumba, lord
  of Palmares, kingdom
of one hundred years;
  Huachinango;

Kishee; King Benkos
  of the golden dagger;
Amazonian Filippa;
  Guillermo of Ocoyta;

Santiago, trickster, wore
  a two-colour hat
between the crowns of France
  and Spain; Yanga;

Bordebois; Fabulé;
  Juan de Serras;
Mingoe of Virginia; Nanny,
  strong in magic;

Captain Lemba; warriors
    of the Cypress Swamp,
the Armadillo's Hole, le Maniel,
    sill of revolution.

Mi ben skrifi da tori
    vo dem ouloetem
avoo vo wi. Let us reach
    further than heritage,

beyond all oppressions, flawed
    treaties, limits
of time and country (what end
    to our roads

of destiny?): to build anew,
    on whichever continent,
the true and sacred city
    we dream of.

VIII

¶ Rafters of the house
sleep without turning.
A year's cadence, blue
  with hoar-frost.

If the eye of night blinks
  between worlds
   seen, unseen,
if our broken tongue
  recalls a purer vowel,

the twofold distance
of this chosen world
and mis-chosen birth-place
  finds return.

Wa kuna nkongo!
Ancestral land of Congo!

¶ Those further than memory,
  those not yet
unnamed, who step beyond
  time's each

to eternity's all, soul
  without interval,

those who in death traverse
  once more an ocean's
denial, those to whom ocean
  was unknown,

ancestral spirits, beyond
      yet seemingly
tented in shadow – grass-blade
      shelters a minute's

elsewhere – earth's voice,
      frame of tradition,
mother drum resonant
      through a progeny

of humid nights. You who are
      native to an idiom
of incantation in which vision
      and accomplishment

are one, drawing breath
      now with lungs
of the poem, double spirit
      of hybrid face,

mask of the forest, threshold
      of death, standing
at crossroads between red
      earth of the otherworld

and black of this – divinity
      is your before
who go before the living.
      Wa kuna nkongo!

Ndundu kuna Ndundu!
I call the water-spirit,

Ndundu in the pool of Ndundu,
      plunge my hand
in the coolness, invoke
      the white-bellied

dog of Ndundu, howling
       bullroarer at night,
who raise your dead son
        to life, make whole

his severed limb, healing
       rift and decay.

¶   But our being-now is being-
        before. Is it we
give birth to the ancestors
       fore-parenting us?

There are those forgetful
       of what we are,
or those who in skin find
       labelled essence,

false term of another.
       Yet how, earth
pulled from under our feet,
      is the pact between

unseen and seen rebuilt?
       How will ancestors'
anger at self-disbranching,
       self-disinherited,

how be appeased? Let us
       earn our past.

It is through soul's kinship
       with the divine
towards beginning word,
       through person

aligned with ancestral vision
      that we seize
meaning above dividedness,
      that destiny

results: our failing sight
      behind time's
screen reaches to wholeness
      of those before.

Wa kuna nkongo!
Wa kuna nkongo!
Wa kuna nkongo!

Ndundu kuna Ndundu!
Ndundu kuna Ndundu!
Ndundu kuna Ndundu!

IX

Roundhouse, icon of all: dream of the kite and macaw.
The skylight writes a calendar of the sun: cords of tobacco-
smoke bind earth and sky.

Flood split the world in two, so that half was unseen,
unknown until the crossing of one *varón ilustre* to a found
paradise of crystal waters.

Plunge of the heron, felling of red cedar: migrant canoes
made coastward and across in an arc of islands towards
confusion of tongues.

"Language...*compañera del imperio*," Nebrija began his
grammar of empire. Columbus: "...that they might learn our
tongue" –

those at the world's outskirts, Montaigne's natural man,
or Ktesias' cynocephali who make love like dogs.

Père Raymond, son of a butcher, wrote his *dictionnaire
sauvage* to people the militant church with new colonies:
mápoya: 'Diable', manícou: 'renard'.

Fear the armed man: without *nostre foy*, you cannot
ascend to the sky. *Religio nulla, nullae preces inter ipsos.*

They do not pray being ignorant of the names of their gods
– yet after nineteen years' mission he baptised only four Caribs,
three of whom died soon after. You will have no god but me.

Stann Creek, Salybia, Arima: emblems of another
struggle. How will we read the curve of our cheek-bone or this
hotchpotch of landscape, conspiring kapok and tulip-tree?

Roundhouse, sun-crafted. Hocket of egret and ibis, flocking white and red to root and branching of mangrove.

The carvings of Bigistong, created after the Flood, guide souls up-river to seek their ancient birth-place, among the flaming colours of the world-ideal:

one-legged elder twin,
    grandparenting all
    instincts in nature,
    who do not see but speak.

Gate of the Pleiades: time
    of the swelling river:

fish obscure
    to squinting arrow.

Amana, mother of twins,
    who see but do not speak,
who cut the three-note scale
    in the flute, boa of waters
in heaven and on earth.

Sharp-eyed arrow
    fills creel of fish:

gate of Orion: season
    of the sleeping river.

Younger twin, Tamusi,
    whose rattle holds
    spirits of all worlds,
    the mind of heaven,
    who see, who speak.

X

Three times they built
    the city: first
ancestor, Odùduwà
      brought together

the several sites flood
    had disrupted
to the present Ilé-Ifẹ̀.
      Ọ̀wọ́nrín is white;

Ọ̀wọ́nrín is not white.
    Divinities too
travelled, were transformed
    in discovering

America; others are born
    at sea's crossways:
Ogun abandons the hoe,
    devoting himself

solely to struggle; Manja
    spreads her arms
to embrace Caribbean sea.
    (Ifá foretold

in antiquity for survivors
    of Ifẹ̀ a time
of an uncertain world:
    weightless people

halfway between earth
    and otherworld.)
Custodian of a new land,
    Mama Latè

comes to birth; Mali Loui
     enters the forest:
invoking the loa, you cut off
     both breasts,

a cutlass in each hand,
     then emerged robed
in blood, armed with the furious
     justice of Petro,

to lead Boukman's revolt,
     planting the seed
of the first Black republic.
     Powers of many

tongues gather beneath
     a single roof,
in guise of saints, choosing
     sacred days

in the papal calendar.
     It is Papa Gédé,
lord of the graveyard,
     hearing invoked

uncertain lineage, alone
     will heal scars
of ancestral rape, mastering
     alien ghosts

which lie far within.
     Those who disdain
this grafted history, kneeling
     before a prior

nationhood, must not forget
      just how many
have died for these religions,
      must know too

that there is another Africa,
      without road-map
or airport: through soul's flight
      across the waters,

we come, whether living
      or dead, holding
in our hand a calabash,
      to the truer realm

of the divine. There would be
      no loa or orisha
without people. We who create
      a fourth Ifè...

XI

White foam of seaways: macadam-red roads of Ògún. Calabash-tree bears no pumpkin.

Let my sight be sharp, Ifá, to see present, past, future:

Chesapeake Bay, where sails fold like gulls' wings, threshold of the tale of the Companies,

a fate shaped from without, yet held firm in our hand, hand of the *òrìṣà*.

"My Lord," Cochrane to Bathurst, "I enclose a box of powdered arrowroot with a recipe (highly recommended) for your wife," reporting from Bermuda

Cockburn busy (1814), enlisting American slaves as marines, the April proclamation, inviting refugees:

"...Those who may be disposed to emigrate from the United States" – namely Blacks – "...free settlers...all due encouragement."

Six companies in all fought for freedom, Colonial Marines, and Governor Woodford, much later, was "alarmed" at their boast of killing crackers.

"All possessions whatsoever taken by either party shall be restored without delay" – first provision of peace – so some were handed back to slavery, and the British were found to owe $1,204,960 for transported slaves.

But hundreds to Halifax, Scylla lying out in the wet, to contagion, frost and the Poor House (despite the 1000 pairs of worsted stockings shipped from Portsmouth), others to Trinidad:

Albion, William, Carron, Erebus. *Ìbà Olókun*: praise to the sea.

1815, a hazy November morning (the log says "breezes light"), passengers of the Carron disembarked at Naparima, 30 men, 12 women, 10 children, first Merikin settlers —

turned down the rip-off of apprenticeship.

The following year came the Colonial Marines, some with families, both Africans and Americans,

six companies to found six villages, in trackless bush

where the howling lougarou and la diablesse with her cow-foot (seducer of travellers) had free rein before the advent of electrical light. The priority was "security to the public".

Four sheds were shelter for the 574 arrivals — iron cooking-pots provided by Government. The house of the tortoise is on his back.

Many were sick with ulcers, *mal d'estomac*, flux and fevers. Woodford: "I beg leave to suggest that they be furnished with shoes." His dream was a "free coloured English population".

Houses were built, allotments cleared and planted: each head of family held 16 acres: provisions, corn, rice, plantains.

The settlements swayed to the rhythm of sawing-feast, cutting-feast, pounding-songs.

Mount Elvin, site of the Devil's Woodyard; Second Company, boasting Matilda Hill; Indian Walk, named after the Guarahoons, traders in macaws and hammocks; Hardbargain, where wives were swapped for horses; Fifth Company, parish of Brother Will; Sixth Company, where the Rock Springs once were the haunt of a mermaid and her companion anaconda.

These who have gone before: Hamilton, Elliot, Dickson..., names of another.

McLeod the White schoolmaster (engaged by the Merikins) taught children to read, but quitted the settlements on becoming "deranged".

They built churches of cedar, thatched with leaves of the carat-palm, Gamble's purgatory of slippery roads and pagan custom:

"*Imperium in imperio*," the missionary said. There were those inclined to the One and those who kept the Many. Ato, pastor of Mount Pleasant. Neza, diviner of Fort George Road.

African Moses, cocoa proprietor, spoke to his daughter in English only, so as not to "spoil her tongue", and a resident family of giant tortoises strolled about his yard, refusing to be seats for children.

It was Fiffin said: "The dead do not die, but holding a calabash in their hand, return across the waters to Africa." And from the tree above her grave at Indian Walk, a descendant picked a gourd to make his rattle. Calabash: world's womb.

But Cleaver poured kerosene on his wife's Bible, and set it alight, when he found she was "reading it too much".

Within weeks of the arrival (1816), local planters petitioned Woodford to dissolve the settlements – among the petitioners several Blacks and half-castes, some only recently out of slavery themselves.

"I hope," Woodford told Bathurst, "that your Lordship will prevail on the Treasury to pay up, because I've already had to abandon plans for my new Governor's residence on account of these Blacks."

Out-numbered males hunted women on neighbouring plantations, and their farms were overrun with weeds. To remedy this,

Bathurst ordered a ship-load of re-captive women to be sent down to Trinidad from Barbados (1817). "You will allow the settlers," he instructed Woodford,

"to take as wives such of those African females as may prefer such a marriage to being apprenticed in the usual manner." And Mitchell had the honour to report the instant marriage, performed by the vicar, of all but the four youngest.

Ìbà Olókun. Moses said: "Beware the reclaiming sea."

In 1821, 79 more settlers from Nova Scotia on the ship called 'William'.

Hard Time Meeting, first Sunday in August, began the guava season, time to commemorate the end of slavery; rainy season saw impassable roads and jubilant alligators.

Grey gave authority (1846) for the granting of absolute title to occupied acreage. "To have and to hold the said piece or parcel of land...heirs and assigns, for ever."

Ta ni oníbodè? Servant of the *òrìṣà*, servant of the people. *Ta ni oníbodè?* Neza: guardian of tradition, seer of heaven and earth.

And fed up with lack of roads and years of Government

neglect, the villagers of Fifth Company petitioned the Queen to grant enfranchisement to the people of Trinidad,

and still tipsy from her Golden Jubilee, Victoria said: "We'll check this out," and set up a Commission of Inquiry.

"I don't know," Brother Andrews told the Commissioners (1888), "what may further take place once we have good roads," betraying thoughts of empowerment.

But no longer now the luxuriant farms or gardens, the hibiscus borders or bougainvillea. So many have left, planting the seeds of another canto.

(Calabash-tree bears no pumpkin.)

I give thanks for the ancestors, known and disremembered, makers of miracles.

White foam of seaways: macadam-red roads of Ògún.

XII

Trickster Ananse, usurper
    of folktales, glib
dialectician, I marvel
    at your nerve, spider
of the Ashanti, descending
    to mundaneness
from myth: a demiurge
    to rival the high god,
you craft a web between
    earth and sky,
but your penis, you say,
    must now be sent
to be repaired by the guild
    of blacksmiths. Yet,
if our own travel-weary
    spider of the islands
(web frayed, as so much else,
    by the weight of history)
hints at a deeper archetype,
    we still can gather
our grosser self to breach
    boundaries of this
ordered world, build another,
    enlivened by chaos,
space for our growth and art.
    We too can measure
the snake, or ride in triumph
    on Lion's back.

XIII

¶ If the root is weak, the rest
     will topple. The poem
  makes its own tradition,
     choosing its past

  from what might have been –
     boat's furrow
  gleaming white against blue,
     a babel of tongues

  housed in one voice –
     and cutting a shape
  in time itself: saying,
     gainsaying, saying

  again. Not self-identical,
     but junction of otherness,
  past or future, the poem
     is parent and heir

  to itself, the Phoenix, spreads
     rainbow wings,
  leaves the upper air for this
     changing world

  to renew at the turn of time
     spent millennia.
  Peaks are seen; ends
     are not seen. Hail

¶ Isis, lady of Philae, who
     guided by the Jackal

seek out the scattered limbs
    of Osiris, joining them
as one, so that the body
    reborn will not rot,

sospitatrix perpetua.
    Apuleius once payed
homage, Plotinos also.
    Nonnos relates

how the founder of Thebes,
    Kadmos, initiate
of Osiris, carried to Greece
    the art of writing,

σιγῆς ἀσιγήτοιο, speaking
    silence: rounded
and front vowels, consonants
    labial and dental

are brought to Harmony
    in Kadmos' alphabet,
graft of Egyptian wisdom.
    That is the root,

¶   by which to gauge Christian
    error: Commodian,
born-again gangster and first
    medieval poet,

wrote bad verse to peddle
    the faith: disdaining
heritage, anti-philosopher,
    "he fooled others,

first fooling himself".
       Augustine psalmed
against the Donatists; Corippus
       praised God

and Justin II, prime
       outlook of empire.

¶   There is a place where four
       rivers meet
(Dracontius), a plain where
       the spring of life

waters the sacred grove
       of the Sun, haunt
of Lactantius' Phoenix,
       paradise on earth.

¶   Elegiac couplets mask
       truer legacy:

Apostle Philip instructs
       Candace's envoy,
and Juan Latino, Granada's
       'lucky crow',

sings victory at Lepanto
       for King Philip II.
Capitein proved the Christian
       basis of slavery,

thus earning his four editions,
       while Williams' muse –
black skin, white body – salutes
       her western Caesar.

¶   If the root is weak, the rest
            will topple. Hail

Phoenix, self-creating,
          soaring above
the libraries of time.
          In the temple

at Heliopolis, she enshrines
          ashes of her body's
older shape, returns now
          to her ancestral

home, death-born, scribe
          of transformation.

¶   Manzano's thirty years
          index an era.
The sea had stranded me
          from myself, says

Neto, as for centuries I failed
          to know myself.
Yet here I am now, uniting
          space, *condensando*

o tempo. Depestre hymns
          a revolutionary Legba,
mender of souls and true
          opener of ways.

¶   To kindle the interrupted
          light of Isis,
Osiris again made whole;
          to steer a course

between illusory essence
    and Africa's denial.
The poem's work is to bind
    together, tell

loss and surviving, to say,
    gainsay, say again.

XIV

Swaying breeze,
lagoon's diviner
on earth;
swaying gale,
lagoon's diviner
in the otherworld.
Shorn tree-stump,
diviner of the road-side;
twisting *ọ̀gọ̀n*-vine
which divines for those in the forest.

Ọ̀rúnmìlà, I call on you,
     witness of destiny –
     we who are scattered
     bitter paths out of Ifẹ̀.
     The touraco from east
     to west everywhere owns
        a single voice.
     You who after the fall
        of Ọ̀yọ́ are praised
     throughout the world,
        divine cartographer,
     speaker of all tongues,

        Ifá, we call on you.

You who oversee the choice of *orí*
     in the otherworld
     at life's beginning,
     lord of synchronicity,

        Ifá, we call on you.

You who disclose the bias
 of *orí* in two hundred
  and fifty-six *odù*.
 Mender of heads, defender
  who retrieve the head
  which strays among spirits,

   Ifá, we call on you.

You who disclose the proper sacrifices
 to the *òrìṣà,* the ancestors,
 and to Orí – Orí most faithful
 divinity to answer an exiled devotee –

   Ifá, we call on you.

Master of balance, you who make straight
 the paths of fate which Èṣù
  turns aside;
 who bring to earth the word
 of Olódùmarè, just as these
  words ascend to *òrun*
 through Èṣù, master of sacrifice.

   Ifá, we call on you.

You who are the consort of Òṣun,
 lady of waters and adept
 of Ifá, possessor of two hundred
 and fifty-six vaginas.

   Ifá, we call on you.

Wall of the temple of wisdom,
 knowledge of whom
  must always fall short.

Èwí, lord of Adó,
Oǹsà, lord of Ọ̀yọ́,
Èrìnmì, lord of Ọ̀wọ̀.

Màpó, lord of Eléré,
Mọ̀bà, lord of Ọ̀tùn,
Màpó, lord of Ẹlẹ́jẹ̀lú,

    Ifá, we call on you
    to witness these rites.

One who sits in honour,
  child of bugles
    of elephant-tusks,
  child of lush palm-fronds
    which sway and dip in the river,
  child of fire which burns the farm
    but not the deeper forest.

     •

Open, sky, open,
  earth, open,
primeval ocean,
  that sun-soul
find its corpse
  in the caverns
of backward time,
  that the two
together, arising
  to birth, achieve
a single mouth.
  To journey by
a nether Nile, pass
  fragrant oases,
thickets of tamarisk:

above, the falcon
hangs in infinity;
below, serpents
of sleep huddle
at the rim of un-
completed vision.
That my eyes,
blinded by sun-
at-midnight,
are schooled in fitter
sight, a truer
selfhood illuminated,
my voice draw
force at the precincts
of endless silence.

The slender palm tree of Ìgètí Hill
twists and splits into sixteen huts.

My head is Èjì Ogbè:
I arise amid blessings.
My eyes are Òyèkú Méjì:
I arise amid blessings.
My mouth is Ìwòrì Méjì:
I arise amid blessings.
My tongue is Òdí Méjì:
I arise amid blessings.
My teeth are Ìrosùn Méjì:
I arise amid blessings.
My neck is Òwónrín Méjì:
I arise amid blessings.
My shoulders are Òbàrà Méjì:
I arise amid blessings.
My spine is Òkànràn Méjì:
I arise amid blessings.
My heart is Ògúndá Méjì:

I arise amid blessings.
My hands are Ọ̀sá Méjì:
    I arise amid blessings.
My fingers are Ìká Méjì:
    I arise amid blessings.
My belly is Òtúúrúpọ̀n Méjì:
    I arise amid blessings.
My genitals are Òtúrá Méjì:
    I arise amid blessings.
My thighs are Ìrẹtẹ̀ Méjì:
    I arise amid blessings.
My knees are Ọ̀sẹ́ Méjì:
    I arise amid blessings.
The soles of my feet are Òfún Méjì:
    I arise amid blessings.

•

Swaying breeze,
lagoon's diviner
on earth;
swaying gale,
lagoon's diviner
in the otherworld.
Shorn tree-stump,
diviner of the road-side;
twisting *ọ̀gọ̀n*-vine
which divines for those in the forest.

Ọ̀rúnmìlà, I call on you,
    scribe of destiny,
        divine circle which alters our death-day,
        one who transcends medicine.

Praise to the Akọ́dá,
    first in creation.

Praise to the Aṣẹ̀dá,
      second in creation.
Praise to Olódùmarè,
      owner of this day.

Let our spirit be aligned
      with the *àṣẹ* of Èṣù,
that our will is directed
      to accomplishment:

to the north, *ẹfun*,
      chalk's whiteness,
to the east, *osùn*,
      red camwood,
to the south, *omi*,
      purity of water,
to the west, *ìyẹ̀rẹ̀*,
      yellow signatures of Ifá.

Divert forces of chaos from us.
      Protect us that we may gather next year.
      May we be blessed with your healing and grace.

Swaying breeze,
lagoon's diviner
on earth;
swaying gale,
lagoon's diviner
in the otherworld.
Shorn tree-stump,
diviner of the road-side;
twisting *ògòn*-vine
which divines for those in the forest.

XV

A fanfare, a silence, a name which is
       no name. You, too, enter
this pageant, John Blanke, trickster,
       trumpeter of nothingness,

mounted on a grey horse. If I try
       to know you through music
mute five hundred years, trace you
       in bitonal haze of a mis-

pitched part, I find only a white
       sheet of paper, another's
to inscribe. Minstrel to the Tudor court,
       salaried 8d a day,

Οὖτις – *le néant musicien.*
       Mouth speaks; hand writes:
redeemed by the Almighty for two
       yards of cloth, Gronniosaw

opened a book and listened, waiting
       for the words to speak,
for a borrowed god of empire
       to circumscribe him in English.

(Fallen Ọ̀yọ́ sowed a scattered
       dream.) Sylvester Williams,
poor boy from Arouca, called
       to the bar at Gray's Inn,

believed Her Majesty's colonies
       could see 'light and liberty',
if he lobbied Parliament with enough
       vigour – not put off

his pan-African stride by the Basuto
      chief who (it is said)
declared that Williams was no African
      if he lacked a language.

Thus the infant steps of a movement,
      caught for a century
between two poles: Horton's progress,
      dialectic of CLR

and Blyden's soul of a race, ordained
      by nature: Crummell
called it permanent essence, and Lewis
      priest of karnackery,

was first to bring to light Egypt's
      colonies in America,
Greece and Rome. If now we count
      achievement of asserted

nation (the riddle of Nkrumah
      bisects the century),
we know, too, nation's unreason,
      famine, genocide,

how tropes of race, countering race,
      whether Napoleonic
fantasy in Harlem, or the confusions
      of blackness in Dakar,

miss the chance of reaching beyond
      premiss of conflict.
The time for the rhetoric and romance
      of oneness is over.

XVI

From whatever then has passed,
    I draw strength:
cry of the *benu* from its perch
    in the willow,
and the Nile rises to flood...
    So that turning
leaves of my memory, I board
    a ship, 'Our Lady
of the Conception', seek harbour
    in Chesapeake Bay;
the dog of old Haiti
    withdraws to the forest,
and Bida's blood drips fresh
    on the sand. Friends,
let us be free to make the world
    we dream of.
If the green-backed heron
    boards the canoe,
there will be strong rains tonight.

NOTES

I (p 11)

Readers unfamiliar with traditions of Yoruba religion (reflected in cantos I, IV, X and XIV) might consult two general works: Abimbọla 1997 and Idowu 1962. In canto I, material is borrowed from two Yoruba divination texts collected by William Bascom [Bascom 1993: 346-351; 1969: 346-351].

Ilé-Ifẹ̀: the sacred city of the Yoruba, both the reputed source of spiritual traditions and the mythic place of origin of mankind.

Ọ̀ṣun (p 12): female *òrìṣà* (divinity) of the river of the same name in Yorubaland.

Ifá...Ọ̀rúnmìlà: two names of the same *òrìṣà* of destiny and divination.

love-shrine: a translation of the pun *ìdí Ọ̀ṣun*, which occurs in the sixteen cowries text referred to above [Bascom 1993: 348, 350].

Egúngún: ancestral masquerade.

chameleon (p 13): *agẹmọ*. An account of the *òrìṣà* is given by Drewal [1992].

Èṣù Bàrágbó...: a quotation of a sacred song from the repertory of the Trinidadian diviner Ebenezer Elliot ('Papa Neza') collected by Maureen Warner-Lewis [Warner-Lewis 1994: 37].

Èṣù: *òrìṣà* responsible for communication between heaven and earth.

II (p 14)

Cantos II and V form a pair: both deal with medieval geography, canto II in the European setting, canto V in the Arab. The more legendary aspects of this geography prefigure certain modern conceptions of race. In canto II, reference is màde to the Hereford *Mappa mundi*, the earthly paradise, the crusades, and the Conquest of the New World.

The secret of heaven...: This stanza echoes an ancient Syriac incantation in the translation of Naveh and Shaked [Naveh & Shaked 1985: 124 ff].

four rivers flow...: Cf *Genesis* 2.10. The Christian history of the motif is sketched by McLean [1989: 120 ff]. On the medieval theme of paradise more generally, see Patch 1950.

Let the garden...: Cf Albertus Magnus, *De vegetabilibus* VII.125: *Ad aquilonem etiam et ad orientem viridarium sit patulum propter illorum ventorum sanitatem et puritatem. Ad oppositos autem ventos, meridionalem et occidentalem videlicet, sit clausum, propter eorum ventorum turbulentiam et impuritatem et infirmitatem.*

scents be spread: Cf *Song of songs* 4.16.

I shall serve...: Cf the chanson *Que vous, ma dame* by Josquin: *Que vous, ma dame, je le jure, /N'est ne sera de moy servie...*

Duce Dame...: Cf Grosseteste, *Le château d'amour* 794-795, where the context is a treatment of the Incarnation [Murray 1918].

***Passe avant*:** a rubric from the Hereford *Mappa mundi*. See Jancey 1987 [4-5] and Bevan & Phillott 1873 [5].

The *mappa mundi*...: An interpretive summary of the map begins here.

Jerusalem (p 15): The world of the *Mappa mundi* is centred in Jerusalem and extends to a periphery of lands coloured with myth.

Blemmyes: Cf canto VI, p 26.

***el fin del Oriente...parayso terrenal*:** Cf the *Diario* of Columbus' first voyage to America, folio 64v [Las Casas 1989: 382]. Columbus later thought he had located the earthly paradise in the Caribbean region [Morison 1942: 556-558].

Outremer: 'the land beyond the sea' in the parlance of the Crusaders [Shaw 1963].

III (p 17)

The principal source for Taíno myth is the account by Fray Ramón Pané commissioned by Columbus. Columbus' son Fernando incorporated the *relación* of Pané into his *Historie*, a work which survives only in an Italian translation of 1571. Pané's text can be read in translations by Arrom and Bourne [Pané 1977; Bourne 1906]. In canto III, I have also made use of an essay in the interpretation of Taíno cosmology by Robiou-Lamarche [Robiou-

Lamarche 1986]. Taíno proper names are glossed in the poetry itself.

stone collars: On these artefacts of pre-Columbian Haiti, see Lovén 1935 [633 ff].

Coaybay (p 18): the mythic region inhabited by the dead.

Guaccaiarima...Opiyelguobirán...Guahayona...Guanín...Guabonito: The 'gu-' in these names should be pronounced /w/.

Heron's Canoe (p 19): The constellation is identified and discussed in a paper on Carib ethnoastronomy by Taylor, who conducted fieldwork in Dominica [Taylor 1946]. See also Breton 1665 [265], under *iáboura*.

IV (p 21)

The outer sections of canto IV draw on the log-book of a Portuguese slaver, which is translated into English with commentary by Ryder [Ryder 1959]. The middle section enumerates names of ships (mostly slave-ships). Here are references for some of them: **Santa Clara** (Columbus' 'Niña') [Morison 1942: 113 ff], **Swallow** [Plimpton 1929], **Amistad**, on which the famous mutiny occurred [Baldwin 1888], **La Perle** [Vignols 1930], **Clotilde**, the last slave-ship to enter an American port [Byers 1906], **Atlantic**, which carried the first settlers to Sierra Leone [Fryer 1984: 198 ff].

mould of Creole tongues: On the role of São Tomé as a slaving station and linguistic gateway to the New World, see Le Page & Tabouret-Keller 1985 [26 ff].

Antonio Nicolás: See Moreno Fraginals 1976 [53 ff].

ἔσπετε νῦν μοι...: Cf *Iliad* II.484 ff.

Ìbà Olókun (p 22): 'Honour to the *òrìṣà* of the sea.' See Murphy 1993 [1-2].

Ògún: *òrìṣà* of all relating to iron. See Bastide 1978 [253-255].

V (p 24)

The chief works relating to ancient Ghana which I consulted in writing canto V were these: the compilation (in English translation) of Arab historical writings on West Africa by Hopkins and Levtzion, the history of ancient Ghana and Mali by Levtzion, and two anthologies of African epic in translation [Hopkins & Levtzion 1981; Levtzion 1980; Kesteloot & Dieng 1997; Johnson et al 1997].

Bida: The legend of the serpent called 'Bida', mythic guardian of the ancient city of Wagadu, is known through Soninké oral sources [Levtzion 1980: 16 ff; Johnson et al 1997: 3-7; Kesteloot & Dieng 1997: 83 ff].

Wagadu-Ghana: Wagadu is the city of Soninké oral tradition which corresponds to the ancient Ghana of the Arab historians, such as al-Bakri (d 1094) [Levtzion 1980: 21 ff].

Bambuk: the region in ancient Ghana where goldfields were located.

kishwar: In medieval Arab geography, a *kishwar* is one of several regions of the world, the central one of which was called 'Babil' (ie Babylon), comparable in status with the European conception of Jerusalem (and western Europe).

Trismegistos' dome: See the account of the Nile by al-'Umari [Hopkins & Levtzion 1981: 258].

Ibn Yasin (p 25): an Almoravid leader who waged a *jihad* in the eleventh century across the Maghrib [Levtzion 1980: 29 ff].

VI (p 26)

On the conflict between the Blemmyes and Roman rule and on the suppression by Christians of Egyptian religion at Philae, see volume III of *Fontes historiae Nubiorum* [Eide et al 1998]. There is also a valuable historical summary by Trombley [Trombley 1994: 228 ff]. Other sources for canto VI include the classic study of Isiac religion in the Mediterranean by Witt and an accessible account of various aspects of Kushitic culture by Welsby [Witt 1971; Welsby 1996].

One hymn is sung...: Cf the opening of the hymn to Isis by
Mesomedes: Εἶς ὕμνος ἀνά τε γᾶν /ἀνά τε νέας ἀλιπόρους
/ᾄδεται, πολυτρόποις /ἐν τέλος ἐν ὀργίοις.
river-boat...ship of Isis: The annual festival called *Navigium
Isidis* or *Ploiaphesia*, in which a ship was dedicated to Isis, is
described by Apuleius (*Metamorphoses* XI.16) [Griffiths 1975].
Witt devotes a chapter to the tradition [Witt 1971: 165-184]. See
also the fragment by the historian Priscus in *Fontes historiae
Nubiorum* [Eide et al 1998: 1153 ff].
Those above...: Cf Apuleius, *Metamorphoses* XI.25: *Te superi
colunt, observant inferi.*
Anubis and Nephthys... (p 27): See an article on Meroitic
funerary religion by Yellin [Yellin 1995].
Narses: Cf *Fontes historiae Nubiorum* [Eide et al 1998: 1188 ff], a
passage by Procopius (*De bellis* 1.19.27-37).
temple was converted: Cf *Fontes historiae Nubiorum* [Eide et al
1998: 1177 ff], graffiti in Greek on walls of the temple.

VII (p 28)
The *Skrekiboekoe* ('Book of horrors') by the Surinamese Maroon
Johannes King (d 1898) forms the allusive kernel of canto VII
[King 1958]. Excerpts of this work are translated into English by
Richard and Sally Price [Price 1996: 298-304]. See also the
biographical material about King by de Ziel [King 1973: 2-8].

Mi ben skrifi da tori: Cf King 1958 [92].
Gînê: On the conception of 'Guinea' in Haitian Voodoo, see
Métraux 1959 [91] and Deren 1953 [34 ff].
dem plij drom...: Cf King 1958 [116].
Legba Pétro, Marinette Bwa-Chèch, Ogoû Jé-Rouj (p 29): *lwa*
(divinities) in the Petro system of Voodoo. On the role of Petro in
the Haitian Revolution, see Deren 1953 [61 ff].
Ganga Zumba...: On the maroon leaders whose names are
enumerated here, see Price 1996.

VIII (p 31)

Opoku gives a comparative account of traditional African thinking about ancestral religion [Opoku 1978: 35 ff].

Rafters of the house...: Cf the following *oríkì Egúngún*: *Àsùnmáàparadà ni t'igi àjà o* [Simpson 1980a: 50]. On Egúngún, see Adedeji 1983 and Drewal 1992.

Wa kuna nkongo: a Cuban Congo chant (*mambo nganga*), quoted again on p 32 and more extensively at the end of the canto. See Ortiz 1981 [56-59].

in death traverse: The idea of souls of the dead returning across the sea to Africa is widespread in the New World.

earth's voice (p 32): *ohùn ilè* (an epithet of Egúngún).

hybrid face: Drewal discusses the hybridity of Egúngún as expressed in myth and masking [Drewal 1992].

Ndundu: resuming the Congo chant. On the *Ndundu* (a water-spirit) in Africa, see MacGaffey 1991 [83-85].

self-disbranching (p 33): Cf *King Lear* IV.II.34-36: 'She that herself will sliver and disbranch /From her material sap, perforce must wither /And come to deadly use.'

soul's kinship...: Cf Plotinos, *Enneads* V.1.

IX (p 35)

Roundhouse: See Wilbert 1986.

Flood split...: Cf Castellanos, *Elegías de varones ilustres de Indias* I.1 [Castellanos 1955: 62-63].

Language...*compañera*...: Cf Nebrija 1946 [5].

learn our tongue: Cf the *Diario* of Columbus' first voyage to America, folio 22v [Las Casas 1989: 142].

Ktesias' cynocephali: Cf Ktesias, *Indika* 23 [Henry 1947: 78-79]: καὶ μίσγονται ταῖς γυναιξὶ τετραποδιστὶ, ὥσπερ οἱ κύνες· ἄλλως δὲ μιγῆναι αὐτοῖς ἐστιν αἰσχρόν. On the place of Ktesias in the history of notions of 'marvels of the East', see Wittkower 1977 [46].

Père Raymond: Raymond Breton, whose works on the language and culture of the island Caribs are listed in the bibliography (under *Breton* and *Rennard*).

son of a butcher: Cf Rennard 1929 [5].

dictionnaire sauvage: The phrase occurs in the dedication of Breton 1665.

to people the militant church...: Cf Breton 1667 [4] or Breton 1877a [xxxi].

mápoya: 'Diable': Cf Breton 1665 [424] and Breton 1666 [118]. On the actual meaning of *mápoya*, see de Goeje 1943 [9].

manícou: 'renard': Cf Breton 1665 [353].

Fear the armed man: Cf *L'homme armé*, the song parodied in numerous Mass-settings of the Renaissance.

without *nostre foy...*: Cf Breton 1877a [9].

ascend to the sky: On Carib shamanic ascent, see de Goeje 1943.

Religio nulla...: Cf Rennard 1929 [134].

They do not pray...: Cf Breton 1665 [283], under *Ichéiricou*.

Bigistong (p 36): This is the name of an island of rock in the Maroni River in Surinam on which petroglyphs are carved. The petroglyphs form the subject of a paper by Hellinga [Hellinga 1954]. *Bigistong* is the title of a book of verse by me [de Brito 1996].

after the Flood: Cf Carpentier, *The lost steps*, chapter 5, section 27 [Carpentier 1968: 182-183] and de Goeje 1943 [27].

one-legged...: The second half of the canto is a hypothetical translation of the Bigistong petroglyphs. There is an article by me which goes some way towards an exegesis of this passage [de Brito 2000].

three-note scale: See Blair Stiffler 1982.

X (p 37)

Three times...: Eluyẹmi outlines a more complicated mythic history of Ifẹ̀ [Eluyẹmi 1975].

Ọ̀wọ́nrín is white...: This is a quotation of an *ẹsẹ Ifá* (Yoruba divination verse) from the repertory of Oloye Adeyẹla Adelẹkan [de Brito 2004: 33]:

> Ọ̀wọ́rín fún; Ọ̀wọ́rín ò fún:
> a dífá fún nwọn l'ótù Ifẹ̀ Ooyè l'ọ́jọ́ sí.

Ọ̀rúnmìlà Ajànà, aráyérọ́ọ̀rún,
sọpé ìgbà kan mọ̀ sì ńbọ̀ wá o –
ìgbà náà dé tán –
tí ọmọ ènìyàn yió maa fó
l'áàrin aiyé àti ọ̀run bí ẹyẹ.
Ó ní kí gbogbo Ifẹ̀ rúbọ
kí òfò ìgbà náà má bá pọ̀.
Ó ní kò ní bẹ̀rẹ̀ n' Ífẹ̀
àmọ́ òfò náà yió kárí gbogbo aiyé...

Divinities...were transformed...: Bastide has written an important study of this process with particular reference to Brazil [Bastide 1978].

Manja: a Trinidadian variant of the name 'Yẹmọja' (a Yoruba divinity).

Mama Latè: On the Yoruba religion of Trinidad, see Aiyejina & Gibbons 1999 and Simpson 1980b. Mama Latè ('Mother Earth') is an *òrìṣà* of Trinidad.

Mali Loui (p 38): a *lwa* of Haitian Voodoo, who is said to have inspired the Revolution.

Papa Gédé: a *lwa* of Haitian Voodoo, the Lord of the Dead.

XI (p 40)
In the course of the War of 1812, when British naval forces were raiding Chesapeake Bay, scores of Blacks, enslaved in America, escaped to join the British. This pattern of defections was formalised and given impetus when, in April 1814, Vice-Admiral Alexander Cochrane assumed command of operations against the eastern United States: Cochrane issued a proclamation, aimed at American Blacks, which held out the prospect of freedom and settlement in British territories to those who might come over to the British side. Six companies of Black marines were enlisted by the British in this way: they were later incorporated as the 3rd (or Colonial) Battalion of the Royal Marines. Most of the Black refugees who reached British ships, being superfluous to military objectives, were settled in Nova Scotia.

The war over, the six companies of the Colonial Marines were disbanded in Bermuda in August 1816. They were allocated land by the British in south-central Trinidad, in North Naparima (as it was called). This was at a time when slavery was still general throughout the island. The disbanded Corps founded six villages, three of which today retain military names: Third Company, Fifth Company, and Sixth Company. Two other villages were established by former American slaves in the same locality, the first by passengers of a ship named the 'Carron' (who arrived in 1815), and another by settlers from Nova Scotia (arriving in 1821). These Black Nova Scotians had also been refugees from the War of 1812.

Canto XI is based in large part on original documents held at the Public Record Office (London). These primary sources are listed at page 85. I have also made use of oral material. There is a helpful summary of the history of the Company villages in Trinidad (or 'Companies') by Laurence, based on correspondence in CO 295 and CO 296 [Laurence 1963]. British commanders' reports on the campaigns of the Colonial Marines are summarised by Cassell, mainly on the basis of ADM 1/507 [Cassell 1972].

Calabash-tree...: a deformation of a proverb recorded in the Companies by Huggins [Huggins 1978: 95].
Chesapeake Bay: See Horsman 1969 [153 ff] and Cassell 1972. The Colonial Marines were recruited for the most part in the Chesapeake and neighbouring areas [Weiss 1995]. Cf WO 1/141 [5L ff].
sails...: Cf Douglass 1986 [106-107].
Cochrane: Cochrane's admiral's journal for 1813-1815 can be read in ADM 50/122.
Bathurst: Henry Bathurst (1762-1834), third Earl Bathurst, Secretary for War and the Colonies.
powdered arrowroot: Cf WO 1/141 [3R-4L].
Cockburn: Rear-Admiral George Cockburn (not the Governor of Bermuda, Sir James Cockburn). On his activities in the Chesapeake, see Horsman 1969 and Cassell 1972.

proclamation: The text of this Proclamation is widely quoted, eg by Fergusson [1948: 10]. A contemporaneous printed copy appears at ADM 1/508 [579R].

Colonial Marines: There are effective and subsistence lists of the Colonial Marines for 1816 in ADM 96/366.

Governor Woodford: Sir Ralph Woodford, Governor of Trinidad.

"alarmed" at their boast: a misquotation of CO 295/44 [56R].

provision of peace...: Cf Fergusson 1948 [33-34].

hundreds to Halifax: See Fergusson 1948 [10 ff], Winks 1971 [114 ff], and Clairmont & Magill 1976.

worsted stockings: Cf WO 1/142 [166R-168R].

Albion (p 41): Cf Cassell 1972 [151]. Reports from this ship in the Chesapeake (on which Colonial Marines were embarked) are in ADM 1/507 [57R ff]. Relevant muster-tables of the 'Albion' are in ADM 37/5005 and ADM 37/5006.

William: On this ship, see Fergusson 1948 [35].

Carron: Muster-tables for the 'Carron' are in ADM 37/5507, including a list of passengers landed on Trinidad on 27-29 November 1815, the first Merikin settlers in Naparima. Woodford reports this arrival of the ship in Trinidad [CO 295/37: 229R-230L].

Erebus: On this ship, see Fergusson 1948 [11].

the log...: ADM 51/2182.

Merikin: This term (from the word 'American') was used of the ex-marines and refugees who settled in Naparima. In the twentieth century, the word 'Merikin' acquired derogatory connotations of rusticity.

turned down...apprenticeship: Cf CO 295/37 [209R], which refers to refugees settled in Trinidad but not in Naparima.

lougarou...la diablesse: On these folkloric entities, see Warner-Lewis 1991 [175 ff] and Huggins 1978 [60]. John O Stewart has written ethnographic stories based on life in Sixth Company, with introductory discussion of the significance of a novelistic approach to ethnology [Stewart 1989].

security to the public: Cf CO 295/40 [108L].

Four sheds...: Cf CO 295/66 [16R]. Woodford reports the arrival of the Colonial Marines from Bermuda in CO 295/40 [105R ff].

furnished with shoes: Cf CO 295/44 [55L].

free coloured English population: Cf CO 295/59 [58L].

16 acres: Cf CO 295/66 [17L].

sawing-feast, cutting-feast: Cf Gamble 1866 [108-109].

Mount Elvin...: On the names of the villages, see Huggins 1978 [8-11].

Brother Will (p 42): Cf Gamble 1866 [113-114].

Hamilton...Dickson: Hackshaw has conducted genealogical research in the Companies [Hackshaw 1993].

McLeod: Cf CO 295/66 [18R-19L].

Gamble's purgatory: Cf Gamble 1866.

Imperium in imperio: Cf Gamble 1866 [107].

Ato: James Alexander Dickson who became Minister in the Third Company Baptist Church in 1948 and served for many years. See Huggins 1978 [97-98].

Neza: Samuel Ebenezer Elliot (1901-1969), celebrated priest of the Orisha religion. See Huggins 1978 [62-63].

planters petitioned Woodford: Cf CO 295/40 [173R-181L].

new Governor's residence (p 43): Cf CO 295/40 [107L-107R].

Out-numbered males: Cf CO 295/40 [179R] and CO 295/59 [60L].

You will allow the settlers...: Cf CO 296/5 [130L-130R].

Mitchell: Robert Mitchell, a planter with liberal views, held the job of 'Commandant' in Naparima with authority over the Companies (from their inception and for several years after). This job entailed administrative, judicial and social responsibilities. Mitchell gave a unique and detailed account of the early villages in his evidence before the Honourable Committee of Council in 1824-5 [CO 295/66: 15R-25R, 90R-102L].

instant marriage: Cf CO 295/44 [119L-119R].

79 more settlers from Nova Scotia: See Fergusson 1948 [34-37]. Woodford comments of the arrival of these settlers in CO 295/59 [57R].

Grey gave authority: Cf CO 296/18 [96R-97L].

To have and to hold...: Cf Huggins 1978 [101].
Ta ni oníbodè: Cf Warner-Lewis 1994 [38].
petitioned the Queen (p 44): See Anthony 1988 [90-96].

XII (p 45)
For Canto XII, I made use of the analysis of Ananse by Pelton [Pelton 1989].

penis...blacksmiths: Cf Rattray 1930 [106-109].

XIII (p 46)
Canto XIII is a history in miniature of African poetry in European languages, alluding to texts which I have translated into English. These translations are collected in my anthology *The trickster's tongue* [de Brito 2004].

the Phoenix: Cf the poem attributed to Lactantius.
sospitatrix perpetua (p 47): Cf Apuleius, *Metamorphoses* XI.25.
Nonnos relates...: Cf *Dionysiaka* IV.249-306.
Commodian: See Raby 1927 [11-15].
he fooled others...: Cf Porphyry, *Life of Plotinus* 16.
Augustine psalmed (p 48): Cf Raby 1927 [20-22] and Raby 1959 [30-31].
Corippus: Cf the *Eulogy of Emperor Justin II* [Antès 1981].
Dracontius: Cf *De laudibus Dei* I.180-205.
Juan Latino: Cf *Ad catholicum et invictissimum regem Philippum elegia* [Latinus 1573: 10-11].
Capitein: Cf Grégoire 1808 [223-235].
Williams: Cf Long 1970 [vol 2, 475-485].
Manzano (p 49): Cf the poem *Treinta años* by Juan Francisco Manzano.
Neto: Cf the poem *Confiança* by Agostinho Neto.
Depestre: Cf the poem *Atibon-Legba* by René Depestre (from *Un arc-en-ciel pour l'occident chrétien*).

XIV (p 51)

An invocation to Ifá, canto XIV draws on several traditional Yoruba texts, especially an ẹsẹ Ifá collected by Wande Abimbọla [Abimbọla 1975a: 54-67]. The middle section of the canto draws on ancient Egyptian philosophy.

Swaying breeze...: Cf Bascom 1993 [250].

sun-soul (p 53): On the conjunction of Re and Osiris in Egyptian religion, see Hornung 1992.

My head is... (p 54): On the trope enumerating parts of the body in Egyptian poetry ('deification of members'), see DuQuesne 2002.

XV (p 57)

John Blanke: Cf Fryer 1984 [4-5, 460-461].

Οὖτις: Cf Odyssey IX.

le néant musicien: Cf Mallarmé, Une dentelle s'abolit... (from the sequence Autres poëmes et sonnets): Au creux néant musicien...

yards of cloth: Cf Albert 1770 [16].

opened a book: Cf Albert 1770 [16-17].

Sylvester Williams: See Mathurin 1976.

light and liberty: the motto of the first pan-African conference in 1900.

Basuto Chief (p 58): Cf Mathurin 1976 [126].

a movement: On the pan-African movement, see Geiss 1974, Esedebe 1982, and Langley 1979.

Lewis: Cf Lewis 1844.

XVI (p 59)

benu: The ancient Egyptian myth of the benu bears some likeness to that of the Carib astrological heron. The benu is a heron-divinity associated with creation [Kákosy 1982; Rundle Clark 1949 & 1950; Watterson 1996: 25-29].

BIBLIOGRAPHY

Abimbọla, Wande Sixteen great poems of Ifá, UNESCO 1975a

Abimbọla, Wande (ed) Yoruba oral tradition: Poetry in music, dance and drama, Department of African Languages and Literatures, University of Ifẹ: Ile-Ifẹ 1975b (Ifẹ African languages and literatures series 1)

Abimbọla, Wande Ifá: An exposition of Ifá literary corpus, Oxford UP: Ibadan 1976

Abimbọla, Wande Ifá will mend our broken world: Thoughts on Yoruba religion and culture in Africa and the diaspora (interviews with an introduction by *Ivor Miller*), Aim Books: Roxbury MA 1997

Abraham, RC Dictionary of modern Yoruba, University of London Press: London 1958 [repr: Hodder & Stoughton: London 1962]

Adedeji, JA The *egúngún* in the religious concept of the Yoruba, in: *EA Ade Adegbọla* (ed): Traditional religion in West Africa [117-127], Daystar Press: Ibadan 1983

Aiyejina, Funsọ & Gibbons, Rawle Orişa (Orisha) tradition in Trinidad, in: Proceedings of the Sixth World Congress of Orişa Tradition and Culture [180-209], Port-of-Spain 1999

Albert, James (Ukawsaw Gronniosaw) A narrative of the most remarkable particulars in the life of James Albert Ukawsaw Gronniosaw, an African prince, as related by himself, Hazard: Bath c 1770

Antès, Serge (ed/tr) Corippe (Flavius Cresconius Corippus): Éloge de l'empereur Justin II, Société d'édition «Les Belles Lettres»: Paris 1981 (Budé)

Anthony, Michael Towns and villages of Trinidad and Tobago, Circle Press: Port-of-Spain 1988

Appiah, Kwame Anthony In my father's house: Africa in the philosophy of culture, Oxford UP: New York 1992

Baldwin, Simeon E The captives of the Amistad, Papers of the New Haven Colony Historical Society 4 [331-370] 1888

Bascom, William Ifa divination: Communication between gods and men in West Africa, Indiana UP: Bloomington 1969

Bascom, William Sixteen Cowries: Yoruba divination from Africa to the New World, Indiana UP: Bloomington 1993 [1980]

Bastide, Roger The African religions of Brazil: Toward a sociology of the interpenetration of civilizations, tr *Helen Sebba*, Johns Hopkins UP: Baltimore 1978

Bevan, Rev WL & Phillott, Rev HW Mediaeval geography: An essay in illustration of the Hereford *Mappa Mundi*, E Stanford: London 1873

Blair Stiffler, David (recorded and annotated by) Music of the coastal Amerindians of Guyana: The Arawak, Carib and Warrau, Folkways Records: Washington 1982 (Folkways cassette series 04239)

Bourne, Edward Gaylord Columbus, Ramon Pane and the beginnings of American anthropology, Worcester MA 1906 (reprinted from Proceedings of the American Antiquarian Society)

Boxer, CR The church militant and Iberian expansion, 1440-1770, Johns Hopkins UP: Baltimore 1978 (Johns Hopkins symposia in comparative history 10)

Breton, Raymond Dictionaire caraibe-françois, meslé de quantité de remarques historiques pour l'esclaircissement de la langue, Gilles Bouquet: Auxerre 1665 [repr: Teubner: Leipzig 1892]

Breton, Raymond Dictionaire françois-caraibe, Gilles Bouquet: Auxerre 1666 [repr: Teubner: Leipzig 1900]

Breton, Raymond Grammaire caraibe, Gilles Bouquet: Auxerre 1667 [repr: *L Adam & C LeClerc* (ed): Maisonneuve: Paris 1877a, intr *L Adam* (Collection linguistique américaine III)]

Breton, Raymond Petit catechisme ou sommaire des trois premieres parties de la doctrine chrestienne, traduit du françois en la langue des Caraibes insulaires, Gilles Bouquet: Auxerre 1664 [repr: *L Adam & C LeClerc* (ed): Maisonneuve: Paris 1877b (Collection linguistique américaine III)]

de Brito, MA Bigistong: A poem, Darengo Publications: London 1996 (Darengo poets series)

de Brito, MA Byways of Èṣù, in: Proceedings of the Sixth
World Congress of Oriṣa Tradition and Culture [151-155],
Port-of-Spain 1999

de Brito, MA Gods in stone: Interpreting a set of Caribbean
petroglyphs, Seshat 4 (Autumn) [16-23] 2000

de Brito, MA The trickster's tongue: An anthology of poetry in
translation from Africa and the African diaspora, with
introduction, commentary and bibliography, Peepal Tree:
Leeds 2004 (forthcoming)

Byers, SHM The last slave-ship, Harpers Monthly Magazine 113
[742-746] 1906

Cacciatore, Gudolle Olga Dicionário de cultos afro-brasileiros,
Forense Universitária: Rio de Janeiro 1977

Carpentier, Alejo The lost steps, tr *Harriet de Onís*, Penguin
Books: Harmondsworth 1968 [1953] (Penguin modern
classics)

Cassell, Frank A Slaves of the Chesapeake Bay area and the
War of 1812, The Journal of Negro History LVII/2 [144-155]
1972

Castellanos, Jorge & Castellanos, Isabel Cultura afrocubana 3:
Las religiones y las lenguas, Ediciones Universal: Miami
1992 (Colección ébano y canela)

de Castellanos, Juan Obras de Juan de Castellanos, prólogo de
Miguel Antonio Caro, vol I, Editorial ABC: Bogotá 1955

Cervelló Autuori, Josep (ed) África antigua: El antiguo Egipto,
una civilización africana (Actas de la IX semana de estudios
africanos del Centre d'Estudis Africans de Barcelona, 18-22
de marzo de 1996), Aula Aegyptiaca: Barcelona 2001 (Aula
Aegyptiaca, studia 1)

Clairmont, Donald H & Magill, Dennis W The changing
political consciousness of Nova Scotia blacks and the
influence of Africville, in: *Frances Henry* (ed): Ethnicity in
the Americas [73-96], Mouton: The Hague 1976 (World
anthropology)

Daramọla, Olu & Jeje, Adebayọ Awọn àṣà ati òrìṣà ilẹ Yoruba,
Oníbọn-Òjé Press: Ibadan 1967

Deagan, Kathleen The archaeology of the Spanish contact period in the Caribbean, Journal of World Prehistory 2/2 [187-233] 1988

Deren, Maya Divine horsemen: The living gods of Haiti, Thames & Hudson: London 1953

Douglass, Frederick Narrative of the life of Frederick Douglass, an American slave, written by himself, ed *Houston A Baker Jr*, Penguin Books: Harmondsworth 1986 [1845] (Penguin classics)

Drewal, Margaret Thompson Yoruba ritual: Performers, play, agency, Indiana UP: Bloomington 1992

DuQuesne, Terence Squaring the ouroboros: A discussion of two new studies of Egyptian religion, Discussions in Egyptology 33 [141-155] 1995

DuQuesne, Terence La déification des parties du corps: Correspondances magiques et identification avec les dieux dans l'Égypte ancienne, in: *Y Koenig & B Mathieu* (ed): Magie: À la recherche d'une définition, Institut Français d'Archéologie Orientale: Cairo 2002

Edwards, Paul & Dabydeen, David (ed) Black Writers in Britain, 1760-1890, Edinburgh UP: Edinburgh 1991

Eide, Tormod; Hägg, Tomas; Holton Pierce, Richard, & Török, László (ed) Fontes historiae Nubiorum: Textual sources for the history of the middle Nile region between the eighth century BC and the sixth century AD, vol III: From the first to the sixth century AD, University of Bergen, Department of Classics: Bergen 1998

Eluyẹmi, Ọmọtọsọ The role of oral tradition in the archaeological investigation of the history of Ifẹ, in: *WandeAbimbọla* oc 1975b [115-156]

Esedebe, P Olisanwuche Pan-Africanism: The idea and movement, 1776-1963, Howard UP: Washington 1982

Fabian, Johannes Time and the other: How anthropology makes its object, Columbia UP: New York 1983

Fatunmbi, Awo Shopew Fa'lokun The concept of male and female polarity in Ifa divination and ritual, Journal of

Caribbean Studies 9/1 & 2 [67-85] 1992-1993

Fergusson, CB A documentary study of the establishment of the Negroes in Nova Scotia between the War of 1812 and the winning of responsible government, The Public Archives of Nova Scotia, Halifax 1948 (Publication 8)

Fryer, Peter Staying power: The history of black people in Britain, Pluto Press: London 1984

Gamble, Rev WH Trinidad: historical and descriptive: Being a narrative of nine years' residence in the island, with special reference to Christian missions, London 1866

Geiss, Imanuel The Pan-African movement, tr *Ann Keep*, Methuen: London 1974

de Goeje, CH Philosophy, initiation and myths of the Indians of Guiana and adjacent countries, Brill: Leiden 1943

Grégoire, Henri De la littérature des Nègres, ou Recherches sur leurs facultés intellectuelles, leurs qualités morales et leur littérature; suivies de notices sur la vie et les ouvrages des Nègres qui se sont distingués dans les sciences, les lettres et les arts, Paris 1808

Grégoire, Henri An enquiry concerning the intellectual and moral faculties, and literature of Negroes; followed with an account of the life and works of fifteen Negroes and Mulattoes distinguished in science, literature and the arts, tr *DB Warden*, Brooklyn 1810

Griffiths, J Gwyn (ed) Apuleius of Madauros: The Isis-book (Metamorphoses, book XI), edited with an introduction, translation and commentary, Brill: Leiden 1975 (EPRO 39)

Hackshaw, John Milton Two among many: The genealogy of Bashana Evins and Amphy Jackson, Privately printed: Diego Martin, Trinidad 1993

Hellinga, W-G Pétroglyphes caraïbes: Problème sémiologique, Lingua: Revue Internationale de Linguistique Générale IV/2 [115-166] 1954

Henry, R (ed/tr) Ctésias: La Perse, l'Inde: Les sommaires de Photius, Collection Lebègue: Paris 1947

Hogg, Peter C The African slave trade and its suppression: A classified and annotated bibliography of books, pamphlets and periodical articles, Frank Cass: London 1973 (Cass library of African Studies)

Hopkins, JFP (tr) & *Levtzion, N* Corpus of early Arabic sources for West African history, Cambridge UP: Cambridge 1981 (Fontes historiae Africanae: series Arabica IV)

Hornung, Erik Idea into image: Essays on ancient Egyptian thought, tr *Elizabeth Bredeck*, Timken Publishers: Princeton 1992

Horsman, Reginald The War of 1812, Eyre & Spottiswoodc: London 1969

Hountondji, Paulin J African philosophy: Myth and reality, tr *Henri Evans & Jonathan Rée*, intr *Abiola Irele*, Indiana UP: Bloomington 1996 ed 2 (African systems of thought)

Huggins, AB The saga of the Companies, Privately printed: New Grant, Trinidad 1978

Idowu, E Bọlaji Olódùmarè: God in Yoruba belief, Longmans: London 1962

James, CLR Towards the Seventh: The Pan-African Congress – past, present and future (1976), in: At the rendezvous of victory: Selected writings [236-250], Allison & Busby: London 1984

James, George GM Stolen Legacy, Julian Richardson: San Francisco 1976 [1954]

Jancey, Meryl Mappa Mundi: The map of the world in Hereford Cathedral, The Friends of Hereford Cathedral Publications Committee for the Dean and Chapter: Hereford 1987

Johnson, John William; Hale, TA & Belcher, S (ed) Oral epics from Africa: Vibrant voices from a vast continent, Indiana UP: Bloomington 1997 (African epic series)

Johnson, Samuel The history of the Yorubas, CMS Bookshop: Lagos 1937

July, RW The origins of modern African thought: Its development in West Africa during the nineteenth and twentieth centuries, Faber and Faber: London 1968

Kákosy, László Phönix, in: *W Helck & E Otto* (ed): Lexikon der

Ägyptologie IV [1030-1039], Harrassowitz: Wiesbaden 1982

Kesteloot, Lilyan & Dieng, Bassirou (ed) Les épopées d'Afrique noire, Éditions Karthala: Paris 1997 (Collection «hommes et sociétés»/Collection UNESCO d'oeuvres représentatives)

King, Johannes Skrekiboekoe [extract], in: *UM Lichtveld & Jan Voorhoeve* (ed): Suriname: spiegel der vaderlandse kooplieden: Een historisch leesboek [90-119], WEJ Tjeenk Willink: Zwolle 1958

King, Johannes Life at Maripaston, ed *HF de Ziel*, Martinus Nijhoff: The Hague 1973 (Verhandelingen van het Koninklijk Instituut voor Taal-, Land- en Volkenkunde 64)

Klein, Herbert S Slavery in the Americas: A comparative study of Virginia and Cuba, Elephant Paperbacks: Chicago 1989 [1967]

Lacroix, Jean Écriture-spectacle et *imago mundi* chez les découvreurs de «nouveaux mondes», in: *André Lascombes* (ed): Spectacle and image in Renaissance Europe [32-59], Brill: Leiden 1993 (Symbola et emblemata: studies in Renaissance and Baroque symbolism IV)

Langley, J Ayo (ed) Ideologies of liberation in Black Africa, 1856-1970: Documents on modern African political thought from colonial times to the present, Rex Collings: London 1979

de las Casas, Fray Bartolomé The *Diario* of Christopher Columbus's first voyage to America 1492-1493, ed/tr *Oliver Dunn & James E Kelley Jr*, University of Oklahoma Press: Norman 1989 (The American exploration and travel series 70)

Latinus, Ioannes [Juan Latino] ...Epigrammatum liber; De...Pii Quinti...rebus; Austrias carmen..., Granada 1573

Laurence, KO The settlement of free negroes in Trinidad before emancipation, Caribbean Quarterly 9/1 & 2 [26-52] 1963

Lefkowitz, Mary Not out of Africa: How Afrocentrism became an excuse to teach myth as history, BasicBooks: New York 1996

Le Page, RB & Tabouret-Keller, Andrée Acts of identity: Creole-based approaches to language and ethnicity, Cambridge UP: Cambridge 1985

Levtzion, Nehemia Ancient Ghana and Mali, Africana
   Publishing Company: New York 1980 ed 2

Lewis, RB Light and truth; collected from the Bible and ancient
   and modern history, containing the universal history of the
   Colored and the Indian race, from the creation of the world
   to the present time, Boston 1844

Long, Edward The history of Jamaica, or general survey of the
   antient and modern state of that island..., intr *George
   Metcalf*, Frank Cass: London 1970 [1774] 3 vols

Lovén, Sven Origins of the Tainan culture, West Indies,
   Elanders Boktryckeri Aktiebolag: Göteborg 1935

MacGaffey, Wyatt (ed) Art and healing of the Bakongo
   commented by themselves: Minkisi from the Laman
   collection, Folkens Museum-Etnografiska: Stolkholm 1991

Mathurin, Owen Charles Henry Sylvester Williams and the
   origins of the pan-African movement, 1869-1911, Greenwood
   Press: Westport CT 1976 (Contributions in Afro-American
   and African studies 21)

McLean, Teresa Medieval English gardens, Barrie & Jenkins:
   London 1989

Métraux, Alfred Voodoo in Haiti, tr *Hugo Charteris*, André
   Deutsch: London 1959

Moreno Fraginals, Manuel The sugarmill: The socioeconomic
   complex of sugar in Cuba, 1760-1860, tr *Cedric Belfrage*,
   Monthly Review Press: New York 1976 [1964]

Morison, Samuel Eliot Admiral of the ocean sea: A life of
   Christopher Columbus, Little, Brown: Boston 1970 [1942]

Murphy, Joseph M Santería: African spirits in America, Beacon
   Press: Boston 1993

Murray, J (ed) Le château d'amour de Robert Grosseteste,
   Évêque de Lincoln, Librairie Champion: Paris 1918

Naveh, Joseph & Shaked, Shaul Amulets and magic bowls:
   Aramaic incantations of late antiquity, The Magnes Press:
   Jerusalem 1985

de Nebrija, Antonio Gramatica castellana, vol I, ed *Pascual
   Galindo Romeo & Luis Ortiz Muñoz*, Edición de la Junta del
   Centenario: Madrid 1946 [1492]

Nicholls, David From Dessalines to Duvalier: Race, colour and national independence in Haiti, Macmillan: London 1996 ed 3 (Warwick University Caribbean Studies)

Nkrumah, Kwame Neo-colonialism: The last stage of imperialism, Nelson: London 1965

Nkrumah, Kwame Consciencism: Philosophy and ideology for decolonisation, Panaf: London 1970 rev ed

Noguera, Felipe The African millennium: Toward the Eighth Pan-African Congress, in: Proceedings of the Sixth World Congress of Oriṣa Tradition and Culture [140-147], Port-of-Spain 1999

Novanyon Idizol, Gro Mambo Angela Religious unification is the mandate!, in: Proceedings of the Sixth World Congress of Oriṣa Tradition and Culture [79-86], Port-of-Spain 1999

Olender, Maurice [Les langues du paradis: Aryens et Sémites, un couple providential, Éditions du Seuil: Paris 1989] The languages of paradise: Race, religion and philology in the nineteenth century, tr *Arthur Goldhammer*, Harvard UP: Cambridge MA 1992

Opoku, Kofi Asare West African traditional religion, FEP International Private Limited: Singapore 1978

Ortiz, Fernando Los bailes y el teatro de los negros en el folklore de Cuba, Editorial Letras Cubanas: Havana 1981 ed 2 [1951]

Pané, Fray Ramón Relación acerca de las antigüedades de los Indios: El primer tratado..., ed *José Juan Arrom*, Siglo Veintiuno: Ciudad de México 1977 (América nuestra)

Patch, Howard Rollin The other world according to descriptions in medieval literature, Harvard UP: Cambridge MA 1950 (Smith College studies in modern languages)

Pelton, Robert D The trickster in West Africa: A study of mythic irony and sacred delight, University of California Press: Berkeley 1989 [1980] (Hermeneutics: studies in the history of religions 8)

Plimpton, George A The journal of an African slaver, 1789-1792, Proceedings of the American Antiquarian Society 39 [379-465] 1929

Price, Richard (ed) Maroon societies: Rebel slave communities in the Americas, The Johns Hopkins UP: Baltimore 1996 ed 3

Raby, FJE A history of Christian-Latin poetry from the beginnings to the close of the Middle Ages, Clarendon Press: Oxford 1927

Raby, FJE (ed) The Oxford book of medieval Latin verse, Clarendon Press: Oxford 1959

Rattray, RS (tr) Akan-Ashanti folk-tales, Clarendon Press: Oxford 1930

Rennard, Joseph (ed/intr) Les Caraïbes, la Guadeloupe: 1635-1656: Histoire des vingt premières années de la colonisation de la Guadeloupe, d'après les relations du RP Breton, G Ficker: Paris 1929 (Histoire coloniale 1)

Robiou-Lamarche, Sebastián Ida y vuelta a Guanín: Un ensayo sobre la cosmovisión taína, in: *Edmundo Magaña & Peter Mason* (ed): Myth and the imaginary in the New World [459-498], CEDLA: Dordrecht 1986 (CEDLA Latin American studies 34)

Rodney, Walter A history of the Upper Guinea Coast, 1545 to 1800, Clarendon Press: Oxford 1970 (Oxford studies in African affairs)

Rodney, Walter How Europe underdeveloped Africa, Bogle-L'Ouverture Publications: London 1988

Rundle Clark, RT The origin of the phoenix: A study in Egyptian religious symbolism, University of Birmingham Historical Journal: Part I, The Old Empire: II/1 [1-29] 1949 & Part II, Middle Empire developments: II/2 [105-140] 1950

Ryder, AFC An early Portuguese trading voyage to the Forcados river, Journal of the Historical Society of Nigeria 1/4 [294-321] 1959

Senghor, Léopold Sédar Ce que je crois: Négritude, francité et civilisation de l'Universel, Grasset: Paris 1988

Shaw, MRB (tr) Joinville and Villehardouin: Chronicles of the crusades, Penguin Books: London 1963 (Penguin classics)

Simpson, George Eaton Yoruba religion and medicine in Ibadan, Ibadan UP: Ibadan 1980a

Simpson, George Eaton Religious cults of the Caribbean:
Trinidad, Jamaica and Haiti, Institute of Caribbean Studies,
University of Puerto Rico: Rio Piedras 1980b ed 3
(Caribbean monograph series 15)

Stewart, John O Drinkers, drummers and decent folk:
Ethnographic narratives of village Trinidad, State University
of New York Press: Albany 1989

Stichting Volkslectuur, Suriname (under auspices of)
Woordenlijst: Sranan, Nederlands, English, met een lijst van
planten en dierennamen, VACO: Paramaribo, Surinam 1980
ed 2

Taylor, Douglas The Caribs of Dominica, Smithsonian
Institution, Bureau of American Ethnology, Bulletin 119
(Anthropological papers 3) [103-160] 1938

Taylor, Douglas Notes on the star lore of the Caribbees,
American Anthropologist 48 [215-222] 1946

Todorov, Tzvetan [La conquête de l'Amérique..., Éditions du
Seuil: Paris 1982] The conquest of America: The question of
the other, tr *Richard Howard*, Harper & Row: New York
1984

Trombley, Frank R Hellenic religion and christianisation c 370-
529, vol 2, Brill: Leiden 1994 (Religions in the Graeco-
Roman world 115/2)

Verger, Pierre Notes sur le culte des Oriṣa et Vodun à Bahia, la
Baie de tous les saints, au Brésil et à l'ancienne Côte des
Esclaves en Afrique, Institut Français d'Afrique Noire: Dakar
1957 (IFAN mémoires 51)

Vignols, Léon La campagne négrière de «La Perle» (1755-1757)
et sa réussite extraordinaire, Revue Historique 163 [51-78]
1930

Warner Lewis, Maureen The Nkuyu: Spirit messengers of the
Kumina, Savacou Publications: Mona, Jamaica 1977

Warner-Lewis, Maureen Guinea's other suns: The African
dynamic in Trinidad culture, The Majority Press: Dover MA
1991

Warner-Lewis, Maureen (ed) Yoruba songs of Trinidad, Karnak
House: London 1994

Warner-Lewis, Maureen Trinidad Yoruba: From mother tongue to memory, The University of Alabama Press: Tuscaloosa 1996

Watterson, Barbara Gods of ancient Egypt, Sutton Publishing: Stroud 1996

Weiss, John McNish Free black American settlers in Trinidad 1815-1816: A hand-list of names of the six Companies of the Corps of Colonial Marines landed in August 1816 as first settlers of the Company Villages, and the three groups of refugees landed in May, July and November 1815, McNish & Weiss: London 1995

Welsby, Derek A The kingdom of Kush: The Napatan and Meroitic empires, British Museum Press: London 1996

Wilbert, Johannes Warau cosmology and Yekuana roundhouse symbolism, in: *Edmundo Magaña & Peter Mason* (ed): Myth and the imaginary in the New World [427-457], CEDLA: Dordrecht 1986 (CEDLA Latin American studies 34)

Williams, Denis Petroglyphs in the prehistory of northern Amazonia and the Antilles, Advances in World Archaeology 4 [335-387] 1985

Winks, Robin W The blacks in Canada: A history, McGill-Queen's UP: Montreal & Yale UP: New Haven 1971

Witt, RE Isis in the Graeco-Roman world, Thames & Hudson: London 1971 (Aspects of Greek and Roman life)

Wittkower, Rudolf Allegory and the migration of symbols, Thames & Hudson: London 1977

Wood, Donald Trinidad in transition: The years after slavery, Oxford UP (for Institute of Race Relations): Oxford 1968

Yellin, Janice Meroitic funerary religion, Aufstieg und Niedergang der Römischen Welt XI [2869-2892] 1995

Zolla, Elémire The uses of imagination and the decline of the West, Golgonooza Press: Ipswich 1978

PRIMARY SOURCES OF CANTO XI

Original documents cited in the notes to canto XI are listed below. These belong to the archives of the Public Record Office (London) and fall into the following classes: ADM 1: Admiralty and Secretariat papers (correspondence). ADM 50: admirals' journals. ADM 37: musters of ships. ADM 51: captains' logs of ships. ADM 96: effective and subsistence lists (ie lists of men for the purpose of Admiralty accounts). CO 295: correspondence from Trinidad to London. CO 296: correspondence from London to Trinidad. WO 1: correspondence and papers, including material [1/141, 1/142 etc] relating to the 'Expedition to the southern coasts of North America, 1814-1815'. ADM: Admiralty Board. CO: Colonial Office. WO: War Office. 'L' and 'R' in the citations refer to left- and right-hand pages in the PRO numbering.

ADM 1/507 [56R-57L]: Vice-Admiral Alexander Cochrane (on board the 'Tonnant' in the Patuxent River) to Admiral John Wilson Croker, ? Sept 1814, no 101. Covers enclosure of following two items. Cochrane reports the operational success of the Colonial Marines.

ADM 1/507 [57R-58R]: Rear-Admiral George Cockburn (on board the 'Albion' in the Chesapeake) to Cochrane, 23 June 1814, no 13. Encloses following item. Reports the effectiveness of the Colonial Marines under Sergeant William Hammond of the Royal Marines (who had trained the Black Corps).

ADM 1/507 [59R-60R]: Cockburn's order (given on board the 'Albion') appointing Hammond as acting Ensign and Adjutant of the Corps of Colonial Marines, 19 May 1814. Includes a statement of Cochrane's strategy of enlisting American Blacks.

ADM 1/508 [579R]: Printed copy of Vice-Admiral Cochrane's Proclamation of 2 Apr 1814.

ADM 37/5005: Contains muster-tables for the 'Albion', listing Colonial Marines and Black American refugees for 1814.

ADM 37/5006: Contains further muster-tables for the 'Albion', listing Colonial Marines and Black American refugees for 1814-1815. Some of these musters were prepared at sea, others at Bermuda.

ADM 37/5507: Contains muster-tables for the 'Carron', including a list of names of 52 Black American refugees for passage to Trinidad, landed 27-29 Nov 1815: 20 men, 15 women, 17 children. These were the first Merikins.

ADM 50/122: Contains Cochrane's admiral's journal for 27 Dec 1813 to 1 May 1815.

ADM 51/2182: Journal of the proceedings of His Majesty's ship 'Carron'. Records the journey from Bermuda to Trinidad of the Black American refugees, who were to become the first Merikin settlers in Naparima (arriving in Nov 1815).

ADM 96/366: Contains effective and subsistence lists for 1816 for the 3rd or Colonial Battalion of the Royal Marines.

CO 295/37 [209R-210L]: Woodford (Governor of Trinidad) to Bathurst (Secretary for War and the Colonies), 9 Nov 1815, no 131. Reports on the progress of Black American refugees (settled elsewhere than Naparima).

CO 295/37 [229R-230L]: Woodford to Bathurst, 30 Nov 1815, no 134. Reports the return of HMS 'Carron' from Bermuda on 29 Nov 1815, bringing more Black American refugees: 34 men, 15 women, 11 children. These were the first Merikins.

CO 295/40 [104R-111L]: Woodford to Bathurst, 28 Aug 1816, no 189. Woodford reports the arrival from Bermuda on 14 Aug 1816 of 574 more settlers, most of whom were Colonial Marines: 404 men, 83 women, 87 children. He gives a detailed report on the settlements of the ex-marines and refugees.

CO 295/40 [169R-182R]: Woodford to Bathurst, 10 Nov 1816, no 205. Encloses a) Petition of the White and free coloured inhabitants of the quarters of North and South Naparima, 7 Oct 1816 [173R-181L]; b) Governor's Reply [181R-182R]. The petition protests against the presence of the Merikins. Woodford rejects the petition.

CO 295/44 [50R-59R]: Woodford to Bathurst, 31 Jul 1817, no 251. Woodford gives a detailed report on the Naparima settlements, which he has visited.

CO 295/44 [114R-119R]: Woodford to Bathurst, 10 Aug 1817, no 258. Encloses a) return of deaths and births of American refugees settled at North Naparima between 30 Nov 1815 and 5 Aug 1817 [117R] prepared by Commandant Robert Mitchell; b) detailed report of the latter to Woodford of same date on the progress of the Naparima settlements [118R-119R].

CO 295/47 [163R-166R]: Victualling Office to Bathurst, 4 Nov 1818. Encloses statement of provisions supplied for use of the Colonial Marines in Trinidad, dated 20 Aug 1816.

CO 295/59 [57R-72R]: Woodford to Bathurst, 30 Apr 1823, no 481. Encloses a) report of Mitchell to Woodford of 15 Apr 1823 on the Naparima settlements [59R-60R]; b) return of population of American refugees at North Naparima for March 1821 and March 1823 prepared by Mitchell [61R-71R]; c) list of those Merikins suffering from illness dated 14 Apr 1823 [72R].

CO 295/66 [2R-3R]: Woodford to Bathurst, 12 Jun 1825, no 629. Covers enclosure of following item.

CO 295/66 [15R-25R, 90R-102L]: Minutes of evidence taken before the Honourable Committee of Council. Evidence of Robert Mitchell: a) Tue 14 Dec 1824 [15R-25R]; b) Tue 1 Feb 1825 [90R-102L]. This evidence of 1824-1825 before the Council is referred to in the index as the 'Negro character report': prominent Whites were required to give evidence on the question of the role of Blacks in the colony. Mitchell's evidence and his reports to Woodford (listed above) are the most informative accounts of conditions in the settlements in the formative years.

CO 295/66 [306L]: Index to preceding item.

CO 295/152 [158R-172L]: Harris (Governor of Trinidad) to Grey (Secretary for War and the Colonies), 18 Nov 1846, no 94. Reporting on the state of the Naparima settlements (which he has visited), Harris recommends that the Merikins be given absolute title to their occupied lands.

CO 296/5 [108L-108R]: Bathurst to Woodford, 25 Apr 1816, no 87. Bathurst instructs Woodford to take measures for the settlement in Trinidad of the disbanded Colonial Marines.

CO 296/5 [130L-130R]: Bathurst to Woodford, 17 Jan 1817, no 127. In response to the view of the petition (cited above) [CO 295/40: 173R-181L] that scarcity of women in the Merikin settlements is a source of instability, Bathurst notifies Woodford that he has ordered the military authorities in Barbados to send to Trinidad a shipload of re-captive women for settlement in the Companies.

CO 296/18 [96R-97L]: Grey to Harris, 28 Dec 1846, no 85. Grey authorises Harris to grant the Merikins absolute title to their occupied lands (replying to CO 295/152, no 94, above).

WO 1/141 [3R-6R]: Vice-Admiral Cochrane (Bermuda) to Bathurst, 14 Jul 1814. Reports on the raising of marines among American Blacks.

WO 1/141 [13R-15L]: Cochrane to Bathurst, 28 Aug 1814. Further statement of Cochrane's strategy of enlisting Blacks in the Chesapeake area in the War of 1812.

WO 1/142 [166R]: Treasury to Major-General Banbury, 17 Dec 1814. Covers enclosure of following item.

WO 1/142 [167R-168R]: Storekeeper General's Office to Treasury, 1 Dec 1814. Re: 1000 pairs of worsted stockings shipped from Portsmouth to Halifax, Nova Scotia, on board the 'Britannia', for the use of women among the 'Negro population of the American states who may have sought protection from the commanders of His Majesty's forces'. Encloses bill of lading dated 29 Nov 1814.